Photograph by Greggory Poitras

ISBN 978-1-61780-415-1

7777 W. BLUEMOUND RD. P.O. BOX 13819 MILWAUKEE, WI 53213

Visit Hal Leonard Online at
www.halleonard.com

CONTENTS

BATTLESTAR GALACTICA
Theme from the Universal Television Series BATTLESTAR GALACTICA

By STU PHILLIPS
and GLEN LARSON

Majestically

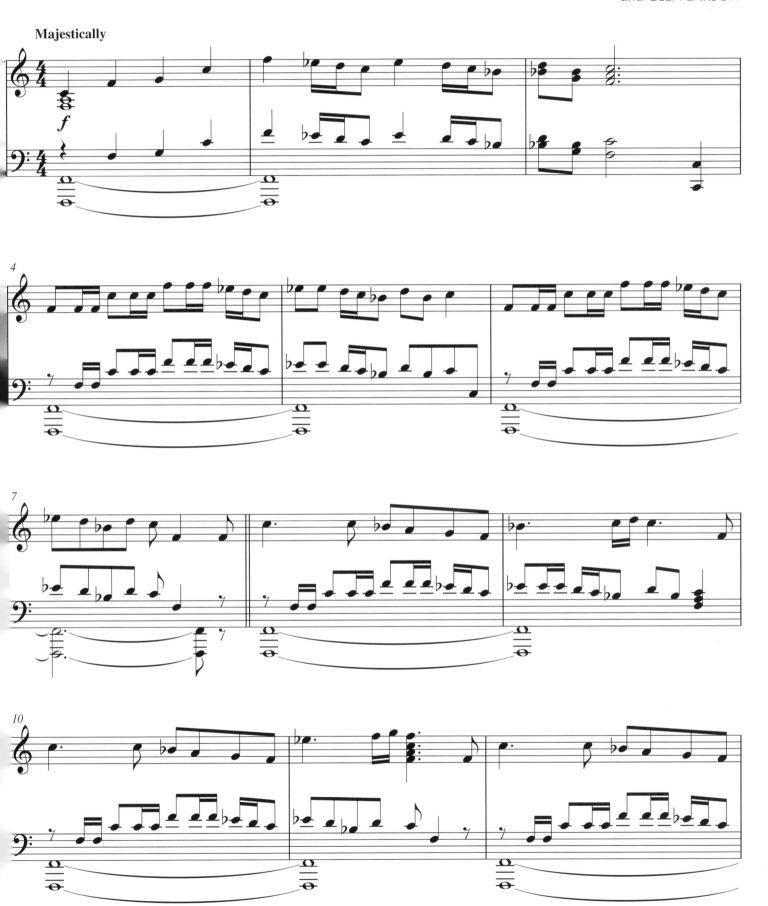

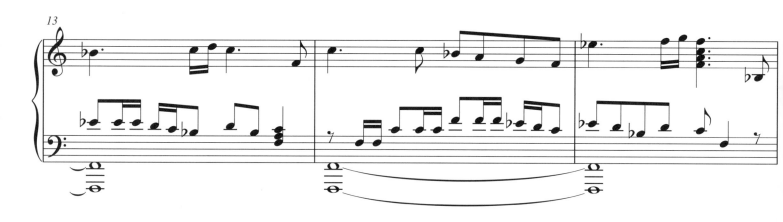

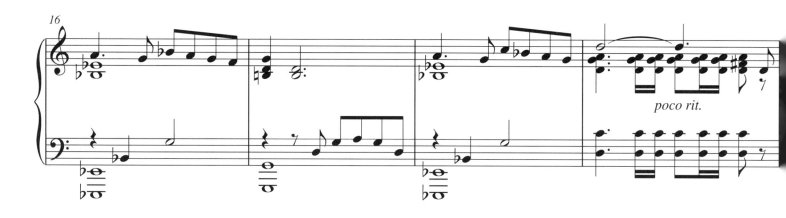

A little slower

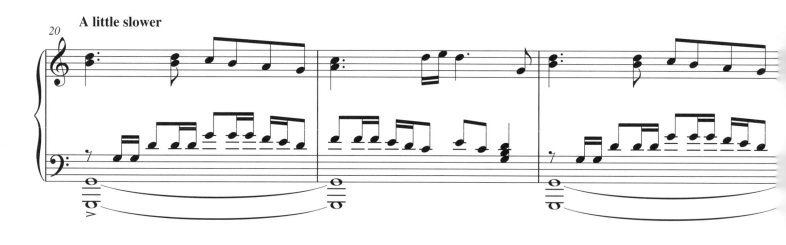

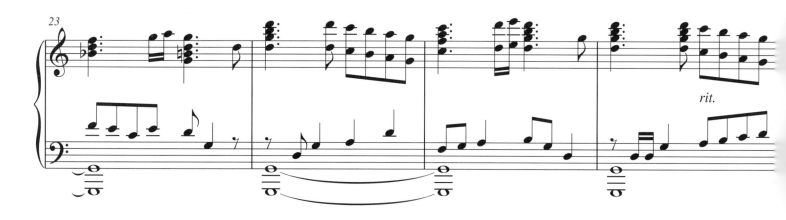

BUGLER'S DREAM
(Olympic Fanfare)

By LEO ARNAUD

Martial, at a moderate tempo

A little faster

CHARIOTS OF FIRE
from CHARIOTS OF FIRE

Music by VANGELIS

CINEMA PARADISO

from CINEMA PARADISO

By ENNIO MORRICONE
and ANDREA MORRICONE

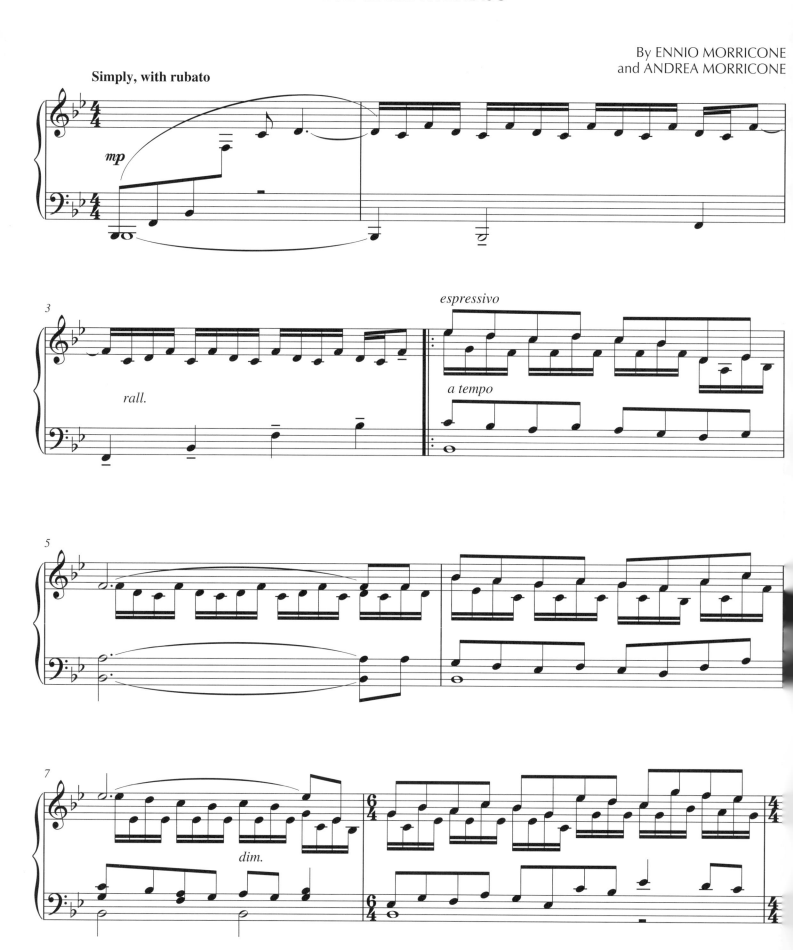

FORREST GUMP – MAIN TITLE
(Feather Theme)
from the Paramount Motion Picture FORREST GUMP

Music by ALAN SILVESTRI

8va

(lightly)

f

THE DREAME
from SENSE AND SENSIBILITY

By PATRICK DOYLE

Moderately, with expression

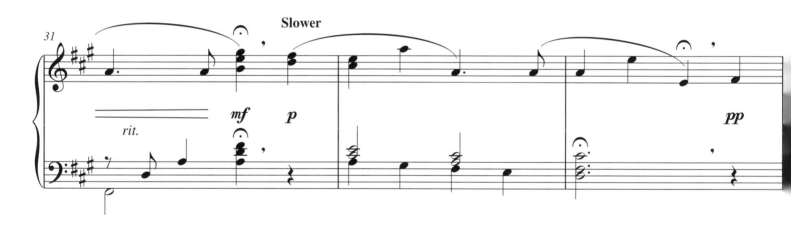

GET SMART

from the Television Series
from Warner Bros. Pictures' GET SMART

By IRVING SZATHMARY

HAWAII FIVE-O THEME

from the Television Series

By MORT STEVENS

With a driving beat

HE'S A PIRATE

from Walt Disney Pictures' PIRATES OF THE CARIBBEAN: THE CURSE OF THE BLACK PEARL

Music by KLAUS BADELT

Briskly

THE GODFATHER
(Love Theme)
from the Paramount Picture THE GODFATHER

By NINO ROTA

Slowly, expressively

With pedal

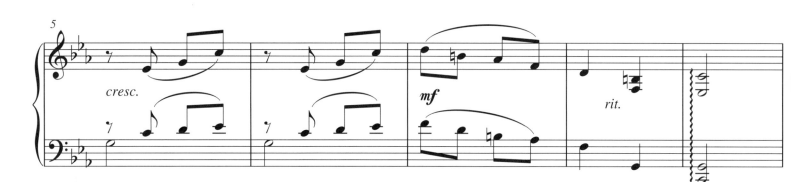

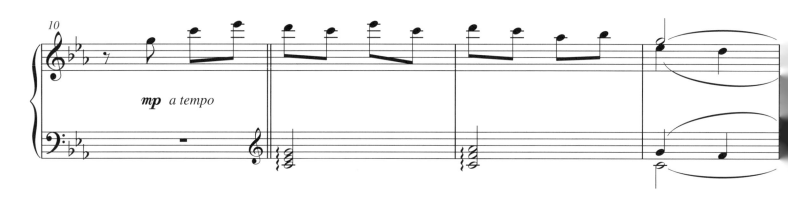

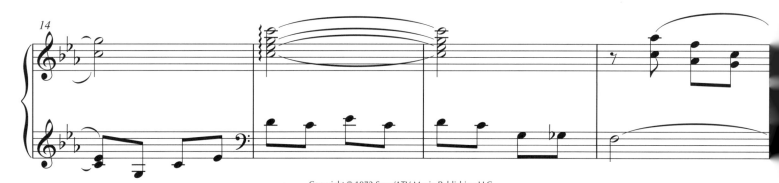

HYMNE

By VANGELIS

Slowly

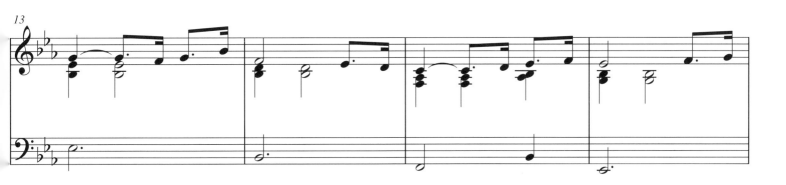

HOGAN'S HEROES MARCH
from the Television Series HOGAN'S HEROES

By JERRY FIELDING

Brisk, steady March

THEME FROM "JAWS"

from the Universal Picture JAWS

By JOHN WILLIAMS

THEME FROM "JURASSIC PARK"

from the Universal Motion Picture JURASSIC PARK

Composed by JOHN WILLIAMS

LINUS AND LUCY

By VINCE GUARALDI

NADIA'S THEME
from THE YOUNG AND THE RESTLESS

By BARRY DeVORZON
and PERRY BOTKIN, Jr.

NEWHART MAIN TITLE THEME

from the TV Series NEWHART

By HENRY MANCINI

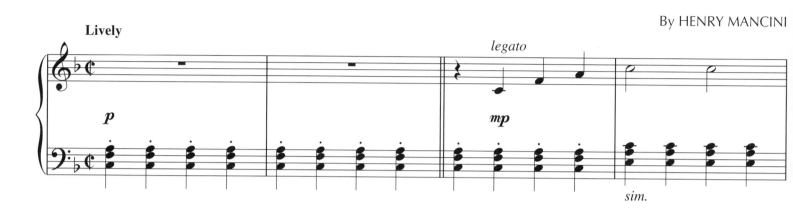

PERRY MASON THEME

from the Television Series

By FRED STEINER

(Bring out bass line)

THE PHOENIX LOVE THEME
(Senza fine)
from the Motion Picture THE FLIGHT OF THE PHOENIX

English Lyrics by ALEC WILDER
Original Italian Text and Music by GINO PAOLI

Gentle Waltz, in 1

With pedal

THE PINK PANTHER

from the Film THE PINK PANTHER

By HENRY MANCINI

Moderately, mysterioso

RAIDERS MARCH

from the Paramount Motion Picture RAIDERS OF THE LOST ARK

Music by JOHN WILLIAMS

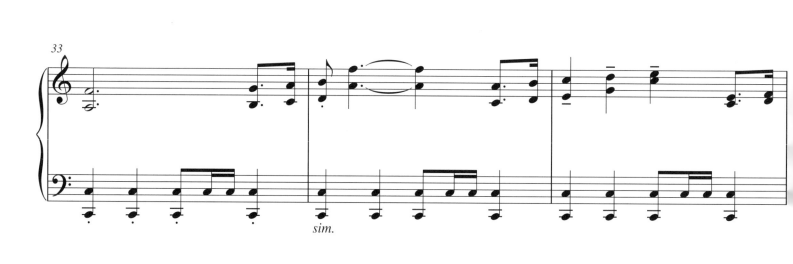

LOVE THEME FROM "ST. ELMO'S FIRE"

from the Motion Picture ST. ELMO'S FIRE

Words and Music by
DAVID FOSTER

Moderately slow

THEME FROM "SCHINDLER'S LIST"

from the Universal Motion Picture SCHINDLER'S LIST

Music by JOHN WILLIAMS

SOMEWHERE IN TIME

from SOMEWHERE IN TIME

Music by JOHN BARRY

Moderately

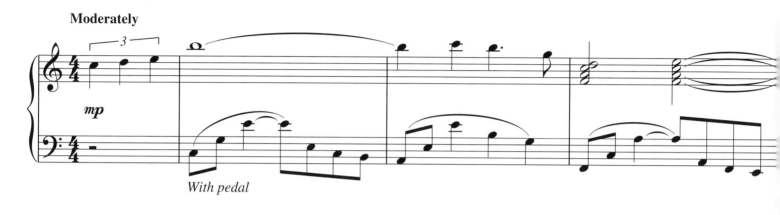

SPARTACUS - LOVE THEME

from the Universal - International Picture Release SPARTACUS

By ALEX NORTH

Moderato

STAR WARS
(Main Theme)
from STAR WARS, THE EMPIRE STRIKES BACK
and RETURN OF THE JEDI - Twentieth Century-Fox Releases

Music by JOHN WILLIAMS

TWILIGHT ZONE MAIN TITLE
from the Television Series

By MARIUS CONSTANT

Mysteriously

bongo cues
(tap on fallboard)

pesante

YOUR FAVORITE MUSIC
ARRANGED FOR PIANO SOLO

ADELE FOR PIANO SOLO
This collection features 10 Adele favorites beautifully arranged for piano solo, including: Chasing Pavements • Rolling in the Deep • Set Fire to the Rain • Someone like You • Turning Tables • and more.
00307585 ....$12.99

THE HUNGER GAMES
Music by James Newton Howard
Our matching folio to this book-turned-blockbuster features ten piano solo arrangements from the haunting score by James Newton Howard: Katniss Afoot • Reaping Day • The Train • Preparing the Chariots • Horn of Plenty • The Countdown • Healing Katniss • Searching for Peeta • The Cave • Returning Home.
00316688 ....$14.99

BATTLESTAR GALACTICA
by Bear McCreary
For this special collection, McCreary himself has translated the acclaimed orchestral score into fantastic solo piano arrangements at the intermediate to advanced level. Includes 19 selections in all, and as a bonus, simplified versions of "Roslin and Adama" and "Wander My Friends." Contains a note from McCreary, as well as a biography.
00313530 ....$16.99

PRIDE & PREJUDICE
12 piano pieces from the 2006 Oscar-nominated film, including: Another Dance • Darcy's Letter • Georgiana • Leaving Netherfield • Liz on Top of the World • Meryton Townhall • The Secret Life of Daydreams • Stars and Butterflies • and more.
00313327 ....$14.99

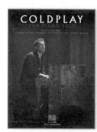

COLDPLAY FOR PIANO SOLO
Stellar solo arrangements of a dozen smash hits from Coldplay: Clocks • Fix You • In My Place • Lost! • Paradise • The Scientist • Speed of Sound • Trouble • Up in Flames • Viva La Vida • What If • Yellow.
00307637 ....$12.99

GEORGE GERSHWIN – RHAPSODY IN BLUE (ORIGINAL)
Alfred Publishing Co.
George Gershwin's own piano solo arrangement of his classic contemporary masterpiece for piano and orchestra. This masterful measure-for-measure two-hand adaptation of the complete modern concerto for piano and orchestra incorporates all orchestral parts and piano passages into two staves while retaining the clarity, sonority, and brilliance of the original.
00321589 ....$14.95

DISNEY SONGS
12 Disney favorites in beautiful piano solo arrangements, including: Bella Notte (This Is the Night) • Can I Have This Dance • Feed the Birds • He's a Tramp • I'm Late • The Medallion Calls • Once Upon a Dream • A Spoonful of Sugar • That's How You Know • We're All in This Together • You Are the Music in Me • You'll Be in My Heart (Pop Version).
00313527 ....$12.99

TAYLOR SWIFT FOR PIANO SOLO
Easy arrangements of 15 of Taylor's biggest hits: Back to December • Fearless • Fifteen • Love Story • Mean • Mine • Our Song • Picture to Burn • Should've Said No • Sparks Fly • Speak Now • The Story of Us • Teardrops on My Guitar • White Horse • You Belong with Me.
00307375 ....$16.99

GLEE
Super solo piano arrangements of 14 tunes featured in *Glee*: As If We Never Said Goodbye • Beautiful • Blackbird • Don't Stop Believin' • Dream On • Fix You • Hello • I Dreamed a Dream • Landslide • Rolling in the Deep • Sway • (I've Had) The Time of My Life • To Sir, With Love • Uptown Girl.
00312654 ....$14.99

TWILIGHT – THE SCORE
by Carter Burwell
Here are piano solo arrangements of music Burwell composed for this film, including the achingly beautiful "Bella's Lullaby" and ten more pieces: Dinner with His Family • Edward at Her Bed • I Dreamt of Edward • I Would Be the Meal • Phascination Phase • Stuck Here like Mom • Tracking • Who Are They? • and more.
00313440 ....$14.99

GREAT PIANO SOLOS
A diverse collection of music designed to give pianists hours of enjoyment. 45 pieces, including: Adagio for Strings • Ain't Misbehavin' • Bluesette • Canon in D • Clair de Lune • Do-Re-Mi • Don't Know Why • The Entertainer • Fur Elise • Have I Told You Lately • Memory • Misty • My Heart Will Go On • My Way • Unchained Melody • Your Song • and more.
00311273 ....$14.95

UP
Music by Michael Giacchino
Piano solo arrangements of 13 pieces from Pixar's mammoth animated hit: Carl Goes Up • It's Just a House • Kevin Beak'n • Married Life • Memories Can Weigh You Down • The Nickel Tour • Paradise Found • The Small Mailman Returns • The Spirit of Adventure • Stuff We Did • We're in the Club Now • and more, plus a special section of full-color artwork from the film!
00313471 ....$14.99

GREAT THEMES FOR PIANO SOLO
Nearly 30 rich arrangements of popular themes from movies and TV shows, including: Bella's Lullaby • Chariots of Fire • Cinema Paradiso • The Godfather (Love Theme) • Hawaii Five-O Theme • Theme from "Jaws" • Theme from "Jurassic Park" • Linus and Lucy • The Pink Panther • Twilight Zone Main Title • and more.
00312102 ....$14.99

Prices, content, and availability subject to change without notice.
Disney characters and artwork © Disney Enterprises, Inc.

HAL•LEONARD® CORPORATION
7777 W. BLUEMOUND RD. P.O. BOX 13819 MILWAUKEE, WI 53213

www.halleonard.com

0812